Native Americans

Shawnee Indians

Caryn Yacowitz

Heinemann Library
Chicago, Illinois

Photo research by Alan Gottlieb
Production by Que-Net Media
Printed and bound in the United States by Lake Book Manufacturing, Inc.

07 06 05 04 03
10 9 8 7 6 5 4 3 2 1

Library of Congress Cataloging-in-Publication Data
Yacowitz, Caryn.
    Shawnee Indians / Caryn Yacowitz.
        v. cm. -- (Native Americans)
Includes bibliographical references and index.
Contents: Land of forests and rivers -- On the move -- Planting,
hunting, and gathering -- Homes and villages -- Clothing -- Shawnee
bands and clans -- A Shawnee story -- Ceremonies and moons -- Games and
contests -- Settlers arrive -- Tecumseh -- Hard times -- The Shawnees
today -- Looking to the future.
    ISBN 1-4034-0867-X (lib. bdg.) -- ISBN 1-4034-4175-8 (pbk.)
    1. Shawnee Indians--History--Juvenile literature. 2. Shawnee
Indians--Social life and customs--Juvenile literature. [1. Shawnee
Indians. 2. Indians of North America--East (U.S.)] I. Title. II. Native
Americans (Heinemann Library (Firm))
    E99.S35Y33 2003
    974.004'973--dc21
                                    2003007476

Acknowledgments
The author and publisher are grateful to the following for permission to reproduce copyright material:
pp. 4, 5 William Manning/Corbis; p. 6 David Wright/Gray Stone Press, Nashville, TN; p. 7 National Anthropological Archives/Smithsonian Institution/Neg.#76-14914; p. 8 Courtesy Afton Historical Society Publishers; p. 9 Library of Congress/Neg.#LC-USZ62-118750; p. 10 Raymond Bial/Urbana, Illinois; p. 11 Courtesy Cincinnati Historical Society Library; p. 12 Linden Museum, Stuttgart; p. 13 National Portrait Gallery/Smithsonian Institution; p. 14 Painting by Hal Sherman; p. 15 National Anthropological Archives/Smithsonian Institution/Neg.#57,125; p. 16 Hugh Clark/Frank Lane Picture Agency/Corbis; p. 17 John Conrad/Corbis; p. 18 Corbis; p. 19 2003 Barry Glick www.sunfarm.com; p. 20 Craig Aurness/Corbis; pp. 21, 29, 30 Lora Nuckolle/Courtesy Eastern Shawnee Tribe of Oklahoma; p.22 Ohio Historical Society; pp. 23, 26 Hulton Archive/Getty Images; p.24 North Wind Picture Archive; p.25 National Museum of American Art, Washington, DC/Art Resource, NY; p. 27 Corbis; p. 28 Courtesy Eastern Shawnee Tribe of Oklahoma

Cover photograph by North Wind Picture Archive

Special thanks to the Shawnee Tribe for its help in the preparation of this book.

Every effort has been made to contact copyright holders of any material reproduced in this book. Any omissions will be rectified in subsequent printings if notice is given to the publisher.

Some words are shown in bold, **like this.** You can find out what they mean by looking in the glossary.

Contents

Land of Forests and Rivers

The land between the Mississippi River Valley and the Atlantic Ocean has very good soil. Today, this is the eastern part of the United States. The Appalachian Mountains reach from the north to the south. Long ago, the area was covered with grasslands and thick forests of maple, elm, and other trees.

Many animals lived there, including deer, mountain lions, bears, wild turkeys, and buffalo. The wide rivers and many lakes were home to hundreds of kinds of fish and waterbirds. Winters are cold and snowy in the northern part of this area. Summers are hot and **humid** in most of the eastern United States.

Areas where Shawnees lived in the past

Shawnee territory in the 1700s

On the Move

Shawnees were a **nomadic** people. No other **tribe** moved as often as they did. No one knows where the first Shawnee **homeland** was located. Some Shawnees think it was in Canada. Others believe it was in the Cumberland Gap. This is a wide valley in the Appalachian Mountains. Shawnees have lived everywhere in what is now the eastern United States. They did not think of one place as home. They believed home was at their village, their dance grounds, and where their old people were buried.

*Shawnees hunted with guns after the arrival of European **settlers** in the 1700s.*

Shawnees were never **united** into one large group. But they were still one tribe because they all had the same language, **ceremonies,** and **traditions.** The Creek, Wyandotte, and the Delaware Indians were often friends of the Shawnees. The Chickasaws were often their enemies.

Shawnees used this tool to grind corn. The corn was held in the bottom part, which is made out of a tree trunk.

Planting, Hunting, and Gathering

Shawnees were planters and hunters. They grew corn, beans, squash, and pumpkins in gardens around their villages. They also gathered hundreds of different wild plants for food and medicine. Shawnees boiled willow tree bark to make a medicine for pain. They gathered wild nuts, berries, honey, and maple **sap.** Spice bush berries were ground up and used for flavoring food.

This picture by Seth Eastman shows Shawnee women at a maple syrup camp. They boiled the sap to make syrup.

Shawnees smoked strips of deer meat over fire. Smoked meat kept for a long time. This photograph was taken around 1900.

Using bows and arrows, Shawnees hunted deer, bears, wild turkeys, and squirrels. Shawnee hunters **imitated** bird and animal sounds so they could get close to the animals. Shawnees showed respect for the animals they killed. They never killed for sport. Nothing was wasted. They used the meat for food. The **hides,** bones, and horns were used to make houses, tools, and toys.

Buffalo Roam

Long ago, buffalo herds roamed all over North America. Shawnees hunted buffalo on foot. The buffalo was an important source of food for them and for other **tribes.**

9

Homes and Villages

The Shawnees lived in small villages. Their homes were made of young trees covered with bark and animal **hides.** Shawnee homes were oval shaped. A smoke hole was cut in the roof. There were no windows. Each house was big enough to hold a large family.

Shawnee Indians and Kickapoo Indians built houses like this one. It is covered with bark.

*A **traditional** Shawnee village looked like this. Someone is building a house on the left.*

Shawnees usually lived in their homes for just two or three years. Then everyone in the village moved to a new area. Each village had a larger house where the people could gather for meetings, celebrations, and **ceremonies.** If enemies attacked, the entire village went to the large house for **protection.**

Clothing

Men and women wore **buckskin leggings** and long buckskin shirts. They wore moccasins made of **elk** or buffalo **hide**. Some men wore cloth **turbans** on special occasions. Dyed porcupine **quills,** feathers, and shell beads were used to decorate clothing. Later, Shawnees traded for silver and beads. They became excellent **silversmiths.** Shawnees thought decoration should be simple but beautiful.

This Shawnee shoulder bag was made in the 1800s. It is decorated with porcupine quills and deer hair.

This is Shawnee chief Goes Up the River. Some Shawnees stretched out their ears like this. George Catlin painted this picture.

In the winter everyone wore fur **robes** to keep warm. Men wore **breechcloths** in the summer. Some men wore nose rings and earrings. For war and for some **ceremonies,** men painted their faces and their bodies. For special ceremonies, men wore eagle or hawk feathers in their hair.

Shawnee Bands and Clans

The people living together in a village were called a **band.** The band was divided into five smaller groups. Each group was in charge of something important such as peace, war, **religion,** health, or leadership. Many villages were made up of people from the five groups.

This painting by Hal Sherman shows Shawnees and other Indians meeting with government **officials.** Leaders from the Shawnee bands were sent to speak with **settlers.**

*Some Shawnee village chiefs were women. Women could also be healers, **warriors,** or religious leaders.*

People also belonged to family groups called **clans.** The people in each clan all had a common **ancestor.** Children were part of their mother's clan. Today, Shawnee children are not always part of their mother's clan. Instead, they become part of a clan that needs more people.

Clan Names

Some of the clans that existed long ago were the Deer, Snake, and Turtle. These clans still exist today. Other clans were the Rabbit, Raccoon, Wildcat, Hawk, Turkey, and Buffalo. Many years ago there were 48 clans.

A Shawnee Story

The Shawnees tell stories to explain why animals look the way they do. Long ago Wildcat was chasing Rabbit. But Rabbit hid in a hollow tree. Wildcat waited outside the tree. He said he would wait there until Rabbit came out. Rabbit hid for a while. Then he said he would come out and be Wildcat's meal. But Rabbit said that he wanted to be cooked, not eaten raw.

Shawnees tell many stories about animals. The animals are characters in these stories.

Wildcats live in almost all parts of the United States. They are also called bobcats.

So Wildcat built a fire. When the sticks were burned to coals, he told Rabbit to come out. Rabbit jumped out of the hole, striking the hot coals with his feet. A shower of sparks flew into Wildcat's face and onto his chest. They burned Wildcat's hair in spots. When Wildcat's hair grew out again, it was white. That is why wildcats have white spots in their fur.

Funny Story
This story was told by the Rabbit **Clan** as a joke on the Wildcat Clan.

Ceremonies and Moons

Long ago, Shawnees believed that every part of their lives was a part of their **religion.** Nothing was separate from their beliefs about life and the **spirit** that created the world. Today, some Shawnees still believe this. They also believe that their dances, **ceremonies,** and religious **traditions** are private. Only Shawnees should learn about them and celebrate them. People who are not Shawnee can respect the Shawnee way of life by not asking about these things.

A full moon comes in the middle of every month in the Shawnee year.

18

The Shawnee name for the month of September is Pawpaw Moon. Pawpaws are a fruit that ripens in September.

Instead of using months, the Shawnees divide the year into thirteen moons. Some moon names are for fruits that become ripe at that time of year. Other names describe the moon during that season.

Shawnee Moons

The Shawnee names for some of the months do not have **translations** into English.

January	Crow Moon	September	**Pawpaw** Moon
May	Strawberry Moon	October	Long Moon
June	Raspberry Moon	November	Changing Moon
July	Blackberry Moon	December	Hard Moon
August	Plum Moon		

Games and Contests

Some Shawnee ballgames are played as part of **religious ceremonies.** Shawnees played ballgames during ceremonies long ago, and they still do this today. Shawnee boys used to play a game called hoop and arrow. They shot arrows through a rolling hoop. This game taught important hunting skills. The Shawnees also took part in running races.

*Running races are still popular today among many Native American **tribes.***

Powwows are not part of the Shawnee *tradition*. However, today some Shawnees go to powwows to take part in dance contests.

Shawnees used to play the moccasin game. They do not play the moccasin game anymore. In the moccasin game, two teams tried to guess which moccasin held a small, hidden object. Each team sang songs to mix up the other team and make them guess wrong.

Settlers Arrive

In the 1500s Shawnees first met soldiers and **missionaries** from Europe. Many Shawnees caught European **diseases** from the soldiers. In some areas nine out of every ten Shawnees died of disease. In the 1600s fur traders and **settlers** came from France, England, Holland, and Spain. The Shawnees traded with them. Soon the Shawnees felt crowded by the many settlers coming onto their land.

This painting shows the Shawnees fighting American soldiers at the Battle of Fallen Timbers.

*The Shawnees lost at the Battle of Fallen Timbers. They signed a **treaty** with the Americans in 1795.*

In 1776 American **colonists** began fighting against the English. Some Shawnees fought for the English. Others soon left the area. They settled in the present-day state of Missouri in 1830. Leaving was hard. But they believed that they had to leave to save their people and their way of life. In 1794 the Shawnees fought American soldiers at the Battle of Fallen Timbers. The Americans won. They took the Shawnees' land.

Tecumseh

As more and more **settlers** came to Shawnee land, the Shawnees became worried. They had a leader named Tecumseh. He cared about the Shawnees and all Indians. His message to the **tribes** was to **unite.** This was the first time that all the tribes were told to unite. Tecumseh wanted the tribes to **protect** Indian land by fighting the settlers together. He wanted to make the Ohio River a border between Indians and the settlers. The settlers would not be able to make new homes beyond the river.

Tecumseh wore a British soldier's uniform for this painting.

This picture of The Prophet was painted in 1830 by George Catlin.

Tecumseh's brother was called The Shawnee **Prophet.** He warned Shawnees to stay away from the settlers' way of life and bad habits. He told them not to wear European-style clothes, not to drink liquor, and not to marry settlers. He thought that if Shawnees could keep their way of life, they would not be beaten.

Sell the Air?

Tecumseh believed some things should never be bought or sold. Land was one of these things. He said, "Sell a country? Why not sell the air, the great sea, as well as the earth? Did not the Great **Spirit** make them all for the use of his children?"

Hard Times

For a while, many Shawnees and Indians from other **tribes** followed the teachings of The **Prophet.** But the United States army began to overpower the Indians. Tecumseh was killed in 1813. With Tecumseh dead, Shawnees did not believe that The Prophet could save them.

A Great Leader

When Tecumseh was alive, some Shawnees followed him. Others did not. But today Tecumseh is remembered as a great leader. He is a reminder of Indian **unity**.

Tecumseh was killed at the Battle of the Thames. The fighting took place in Canada.

Children from the Shawnee tribe and many other tribes were sent to schools far away from their families. This photograph of students at the Carlisle Indian School in Pennsylvania was taken in 1900.

Around 1830, the United States government forced the Shawnees and other eastern tribes to leave their land. They had to move to the present-day states of Kansas and Oklahoma. The government sent Shawnee children to Indian schools. There, Shawnee children had to speak only English. If they spoke the Shawnee language, they were beaten. The government made Indian children dress and behave like white children.

The Shawnees Today

Today there are about 12,000 Shawnee Indians. About six out of every ten Shawnees live in or around the state of Oklahoma. The rest live all over the United States and in other countries. Shawnees are divided into three governments or **tribes:** the Absentee Shawnees, the Eastern Shawnees, and the Shawnee Tribe.

This is the seal of the Eastern Shawnee Tribe of Oklahoma.

*Today some Shawnees still make **traditional** crafts. This is a berry basket. Shawnees used baskets like this one to collect berries.*

Each of the Shawnee tribes works to keep the Shawnee way of life strong. Some Shawnees teach the Shawnee language to children and adults. Shawnee people work in all kinds of jobs. They are teachers, nurses, lawyers, businesspeople, farmers, and artists. Good jobs, education, and health care are important to Shawnees.

Looking to the Future

Today some Shawnee children grow up knowing their **clan**. If they are members of the Shawnee **Tribe** of Oklahoma, they celebrate many of the Shawnee **ceremonies**. Some grow up hearing and speaking both the Shawnee language and English. Although **powwows** are not part of Shawnee **traditions,** many Shawnees enjoy going to them. A Shawnee leader says, "Shawnees believe powwows remind us of how we are supposed to live."

*Shawnee children are taught to respect their **elders**. This Shawnee boy is at a powwow, shaking hands with the singers at the drum.*

Glossary

ancestor   relative who lived long before someone's parents and grandparents

band   group of people

breechcloth   piece of clothing that covers the area from the waist to the knees

buckskin   deerskin leather made soft by tanning

ceremony   event that celebrates a special occasion

clan   group of families that are related

colonist   person who lives in a land that is ruled by a distant country

disease   sickness

elder   older person

elk   large animal that looks like a deer but is much bigger

hide   skin of a large, dead animal, usually with the fur still on it

homeland   place where a group of people come from

humid   when the air feels wet or moist

imitate   copy the way something looks, acts, or sounds

legging   covering for the leg

missionary   person who teaches others about religion

nomadic   people who always move from place to place

official   person with power to carry out rules

pawpaw   small fruit that turns yellow when ripe

powwow   Indian gathering or celebration

prophet   religious leader. People believe a prophet speaks for a god or spirit.

protect   keep from harm or danger

quill   long, stiff spine that sticks out on the body of a porcupine

religion   system of spiritual beliefs and practices

robe   long, loose piece of clothing

sap   sugary liquid in a tree's trunk and branches

settler   person who makes a home in a new place

silversmith   person who makes things from silver

spirit   invisible force or being with special power

tradition   custom or story that has been passed from older people to younger people for a long time

translation   words that mean the same thing in a different language

treaty   agreement between governments or groups of people

tribe   group of people who share language, customs, beliefs, and often government

turban   long scarf wound around the head many times

unite   come together to do something

warrior   person who fights in battles

More Books to Read

Fitterer, Ann C. *Tecumseh: Chief of the Shawnee.* Eden Prairie, Minn.: The Child's World, 2002.

Marsh, Carol. *Tecumseh: An Ohio Experience Reader.* Peachtree City, Ga.: Gallopade International, 2001.

Mattern, Joanne. *The Shawnee Indians.* Minnetonka, Minn.: Bridgestone Books, 2001.

Press, Petra. *The Shawnee.* Minneapolis, Minn.: Compass Point Books, 2002.

Index